HAL•LEONARD
INSTRUMENTAL
PLAY-ALONG

ONLINE MEDIA INCLUDED
Audio Recordings
Printable Piano Accompaniments

Speed • Pitch • Balance • Loop

CLASSICAL SOLOS
FOR
BASSOON

15 Easy Solos for Contest and Performance

Arranged by Philip Sparke

To access recordings and PDF accompaniments visit:
www.halleonard.com/mylibrary

Enter Code
6946-1787-1712-4250

ISBN 978-1-61780-696-4

HAL•LEONARD®
CORPORATION
7777 W. BLUEMOUND RD. P.O. BOX 13819 MILWAUKEE, WI 53213

Visit Hal Leonard Online at
www.halleonard.com

WALTZ

MORITZ VOGEL
Arranged by PHILIP SPARKE

BASSOON

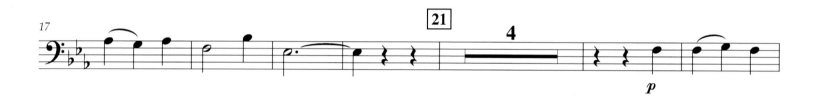

CHORALE

Now praise, my soul, the Lord

JOHANN SEBASTIAN BACH
Arranged by PHILIP SPARKE

BASSOON

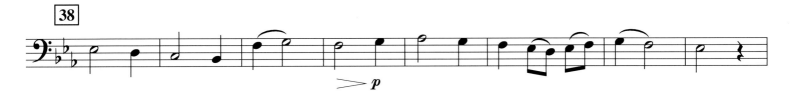

00842544

HUMMING SONG

from *Album for the Young*

ROBERT SCHUMANN
Arranged by PHILIP SPARKE

BASSOON

00842544

GYMNOPÉDIE NO. 1

ERIK SATIE
Arranged by PHILIP SPARKE

BASSOON

00842544

I'M CALLED LITTLE BUTTERCUP

from *HMS Pinafore*

SIR ARTHUR SULLIVAN
Arranged by PHILIP SPARKE

BASSOON

STUDY
Op. 37, No. 3

HENRY LEMOINE
Arranged by PHILIP SPARKE

BASSOON

00842544

MINUET
(Z. 649)

HENRY PURCELL
Arranged by PHILIP SPARKE

BASSOON

THEME AND VARIATION

from *Sonatina No. 3*

THOMAS ATTWOOD
Arranged by PHILIP SPARKE

BASSOON

00842544

NORTHERN SONG

from *Album for the Young*

BASSOON

ROBERT SCHUMANN
Arranged by PHILIP SPARKE

Moderato (♩ = 94)

TWO GERMAN DANCES

from *Twelve German Dances, D. 420*

FRANZ SCHUBERT
Arranged by PHILIP SPARKE

BASSOON

WATCHMAN'S SONG

from *Lyric Pieces, Op. 12*

EDVARD GRIEG
Arranged by PHILIP SPARKE

BASSOON

GAVOTTE

BASSOON

JAN LADISLAV DUSSEK
Arranged by PHILIP SPARKE

00842544

14

VIEN QUÀ, DORINA BELLA

ANTONIO BIANCHI
Transcribed by **C. M. von WEBER**
Arranged by PHILIP SPARKE

BASSOON

00842544

MINUET

from *Notebook for Anna Magdalena Bach*

Attributed to **CHRISTIAN PETZOLD**
Arranged by PHILIP SPARKE

BASSOON

THE PRINCE OF DENMARK'S MARCH

from *Choice Lessons for the Harpsichord or Spinet*

JEREMIAH CLARKE
Arranged by PHILIP SPARKE

BASSOON